MEL BAY PRESENTS

PRAISE FINGERSTYLE GUITAR MADE EASY

BY WILLIAM BAY

CD Contents

1. Tuning Note [1:39]
2. Sanctuary [0:47]
3. Sanctuary (backup only) [0:49]
4. The Lord is in His Holy Temple [1:08]
5. The Lord is in His Holy Temple (backup only) [1:07]
6. Shine, Jesus, Shine [1:13]
7. Shine, Jesus, Shine (backup only) [1:12]
8. Worthy and Holy [1:44]
9. Worthy and Holy (backup only) [1:43]
10. Lord, Reign in Me [1:57]
11. Lord, Reign in Me (backup only) [1:57]
12. He Who Comes unto the Lord [0:53]
13. He Who Comes unto the Lord (backup only) [0:53]
14. Come, Now is the Time to Worship [1:19]
15. Come, Now is the Time to Worship (backup only) [1:19]
16. Draw Me Close [2:11]
17. Draw Me Close (backup only) [2:11]
18. We Love Thee, O Lord [0:28]
19. We Love Thee, O Lord (backup only) [0:28]
20. Holy, Thou Art Holy [1:10]
21. Holy, Thou Art Holy (backup only) [1:10]
22. Bless the Lord [1:45]
23. Bless the Lord (backup only) [1:45]
24. Lord, I Lift Your Name on High [0:50]
25. Lord, I Lift Your Name on High (backup only) [0:48]
26. As the Deer [0:54]
27. As the Deer (backup only) [0:52]
28. Give Thanks [2:51]
29. Give Thanks (backup only) [2:51]
30. Jesus, Never Have I Heard a Name [0:53]
31. Jesus, Never Have I Heard a Name (backup only) [0:52]

1 2 3 4 5 6 7 8 9 0

Visit us on the Web at www.melbay.com — E-mail us at email@melbay.com

Table of Contents

Chords Used

G G7 Gsus C D D7

Dsus Dm Dm7 A A7 Am

Am7 E Esus Em Bm Bm7

B7 F FMaj7 B♭ C♯m Gm

Asus

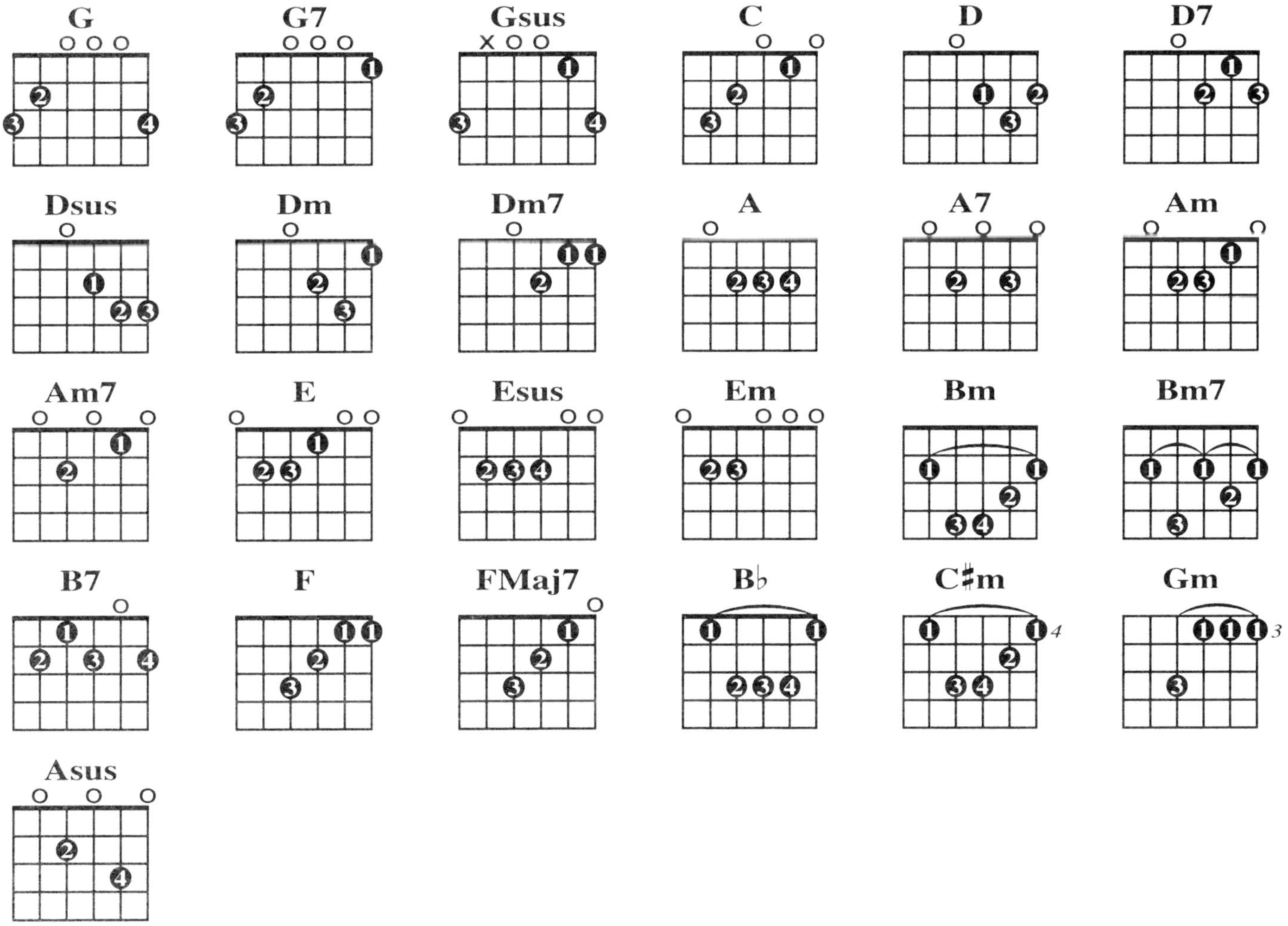

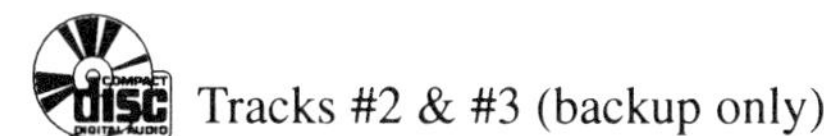

Sanctuary

John Thompson
Randy Scruggs

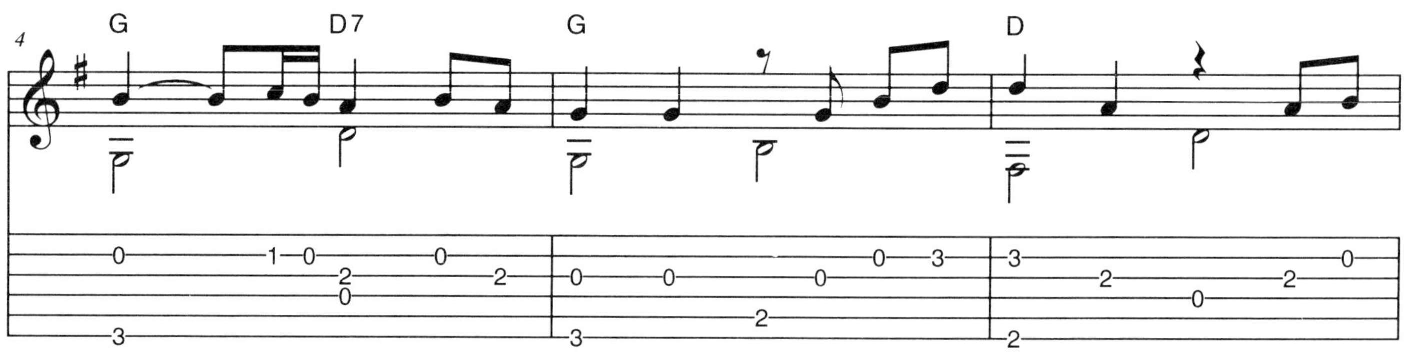

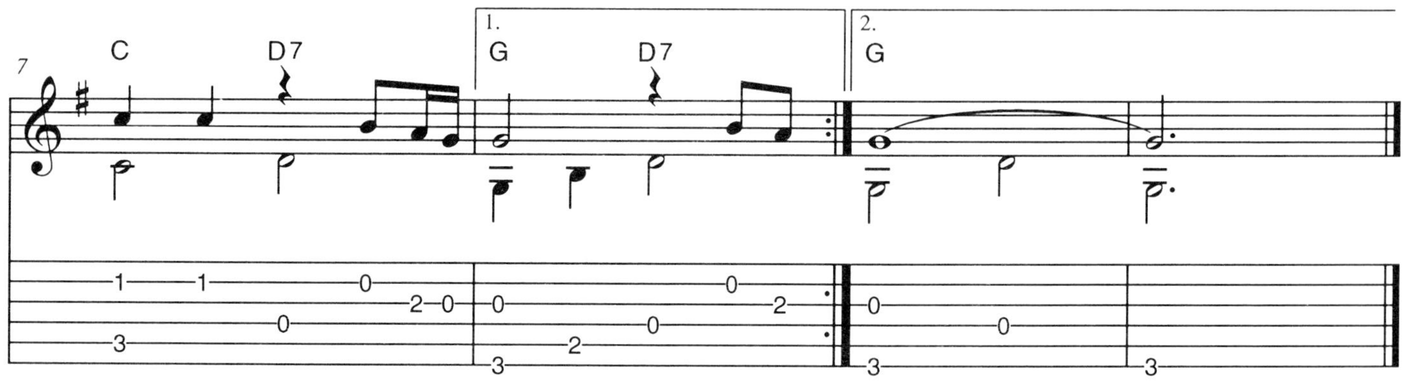

1. Lord, prepare me to be a sanctuary,
   Pure and holy, tried and true.
   With thanksgiving, I'll be living sanctuary for you.

2. Lord, prepare me to be a sanctuary,
   Pure and holy, tried and true.
   With thanksgiving, I'll be living sanctuary for you.

3. Lord, prepare me to be a sanctuary,
   Pure and holy, tried and true.
   With thanksgiving, I'll be living sanctuary for you.
   I'll be a living sanctuary for you.

The Lord is in His Holy Temple

Tracks #4 & #5 (backup only)

W. Bay

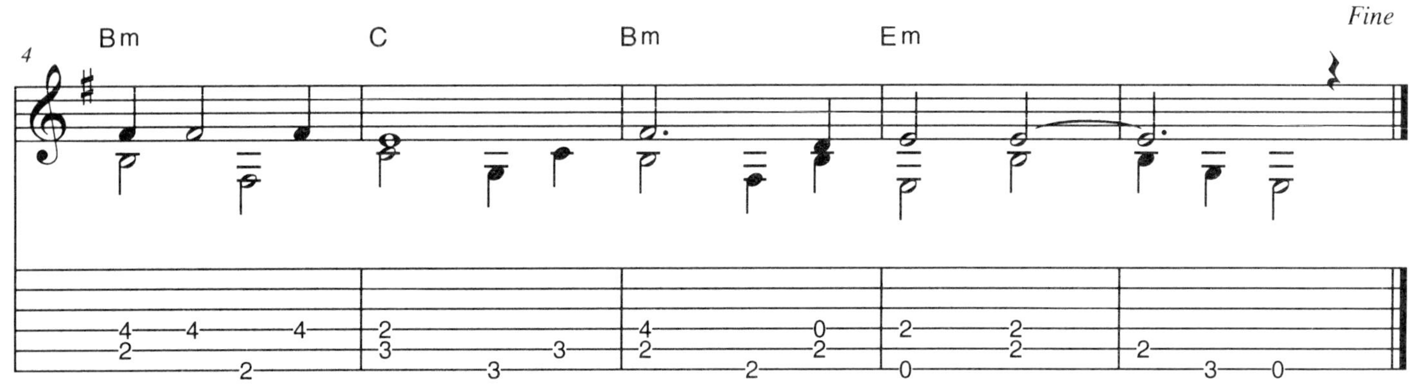

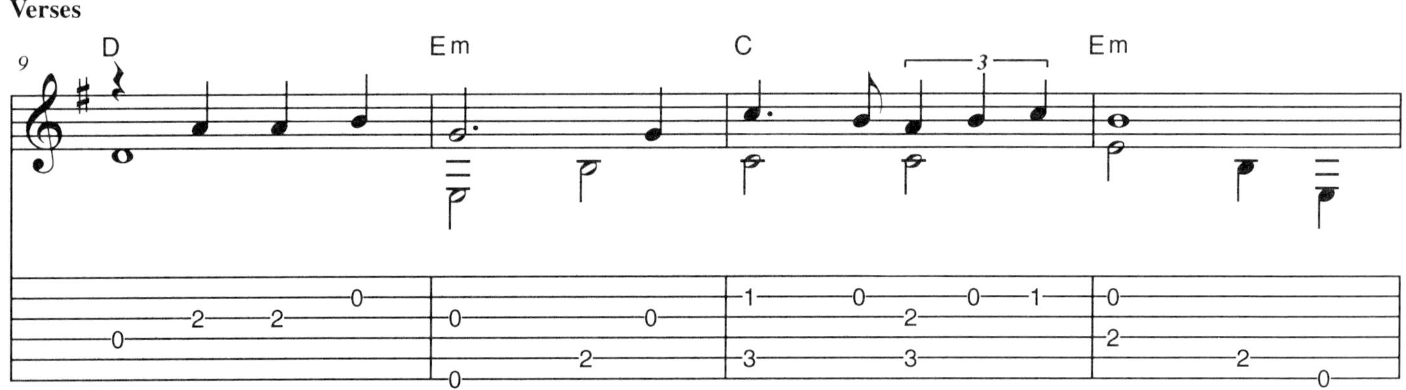

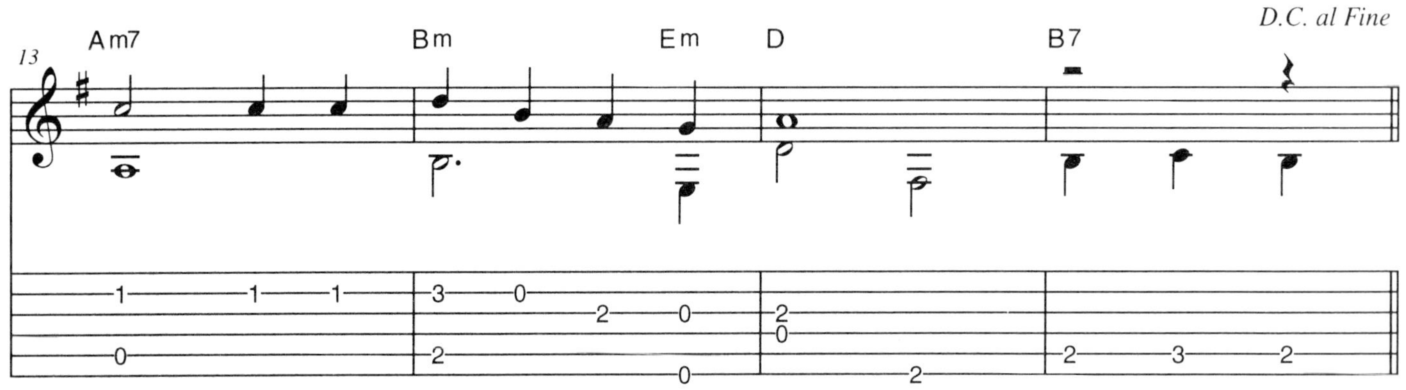

CHORUS

The Lord is in His holy temple;
Let all the earth keep silence before Him,
Keep silence before Him.

1. Who shall ascend into the hill of the Lord?
He who hath clean hands and pure heart.

CHORUS

2. Seraphim cry, "Holy is the Lord!"
Let all creation stand in awe!

CHORUS

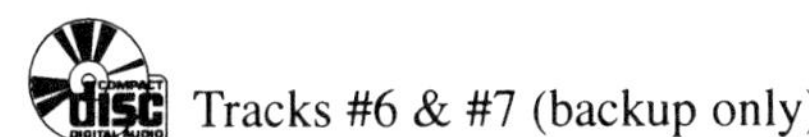

Shine, Jesus, Shine

Graham Kendrick

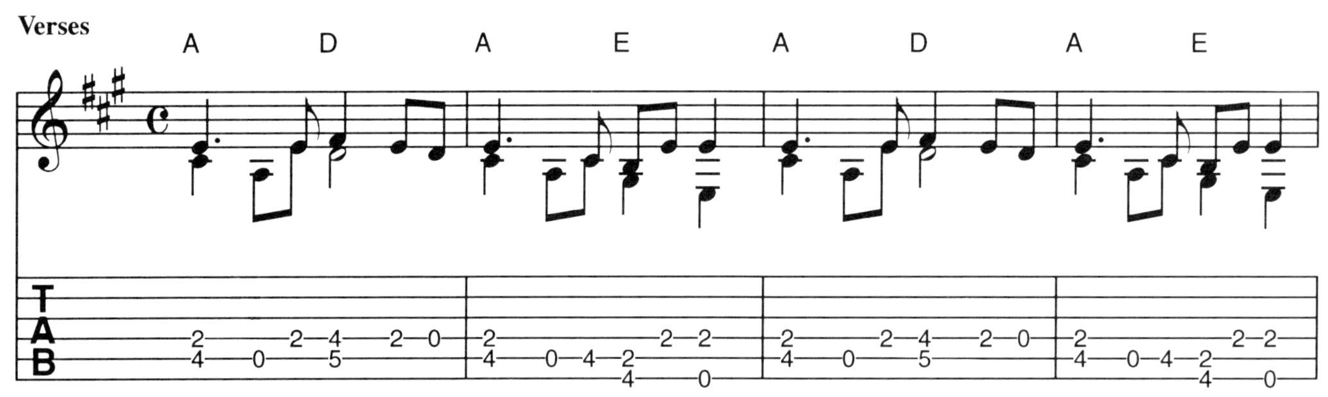

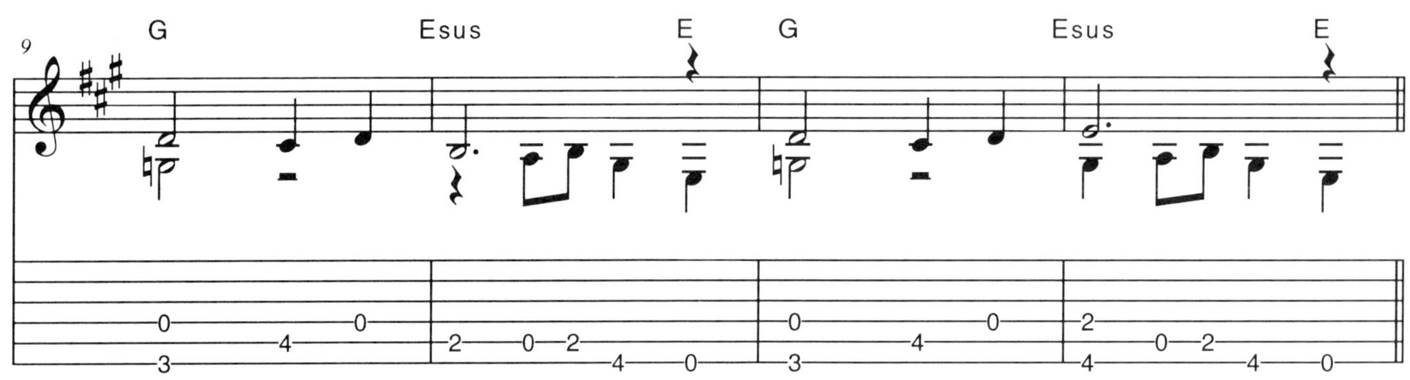

Chorus

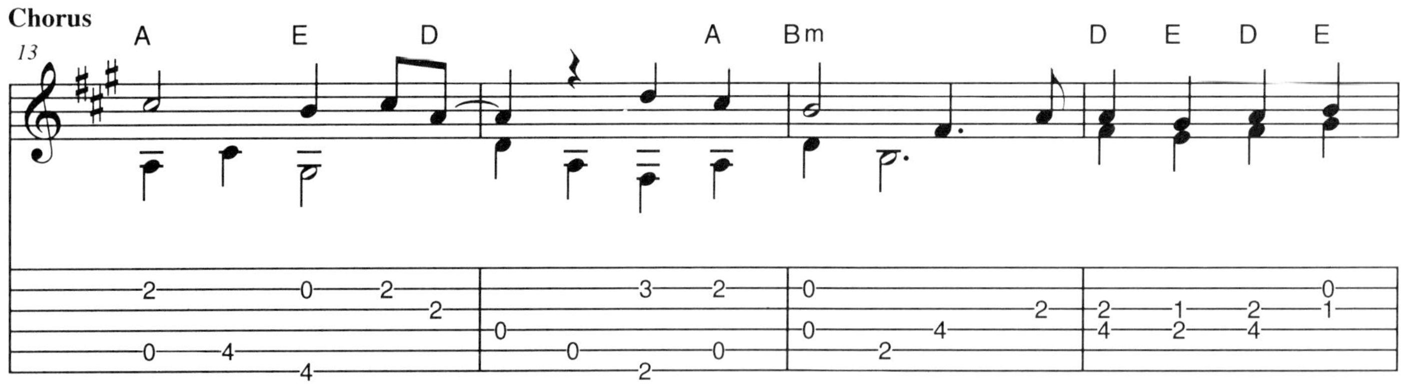

1. Lord, the light of Your love is shining,
In the midst of the darkness shining;
Jesus, Light of the world, shine upon us,
Set us free by the truth You now bring us;
Shine on me,
Shine on me.

CHORUS
Shine, Jesus, shine,
Fill the land with the Father's glory,
Blaze, Spirit, blaze,
Set our hearts on fire.
Flow, river, flow,
Flood the nations with grace and mercy.
Send forth Your word,
Lord, and let there be light.

2. Lord, I come to Your awesome presence,
From the shadows into Your radiance;
By the blood I may enter Your brightness;
Search me, try me, consume all my darkness;
Shine on me,
Shine on me.

CHORUS

Worthy and Holy

W. Bay

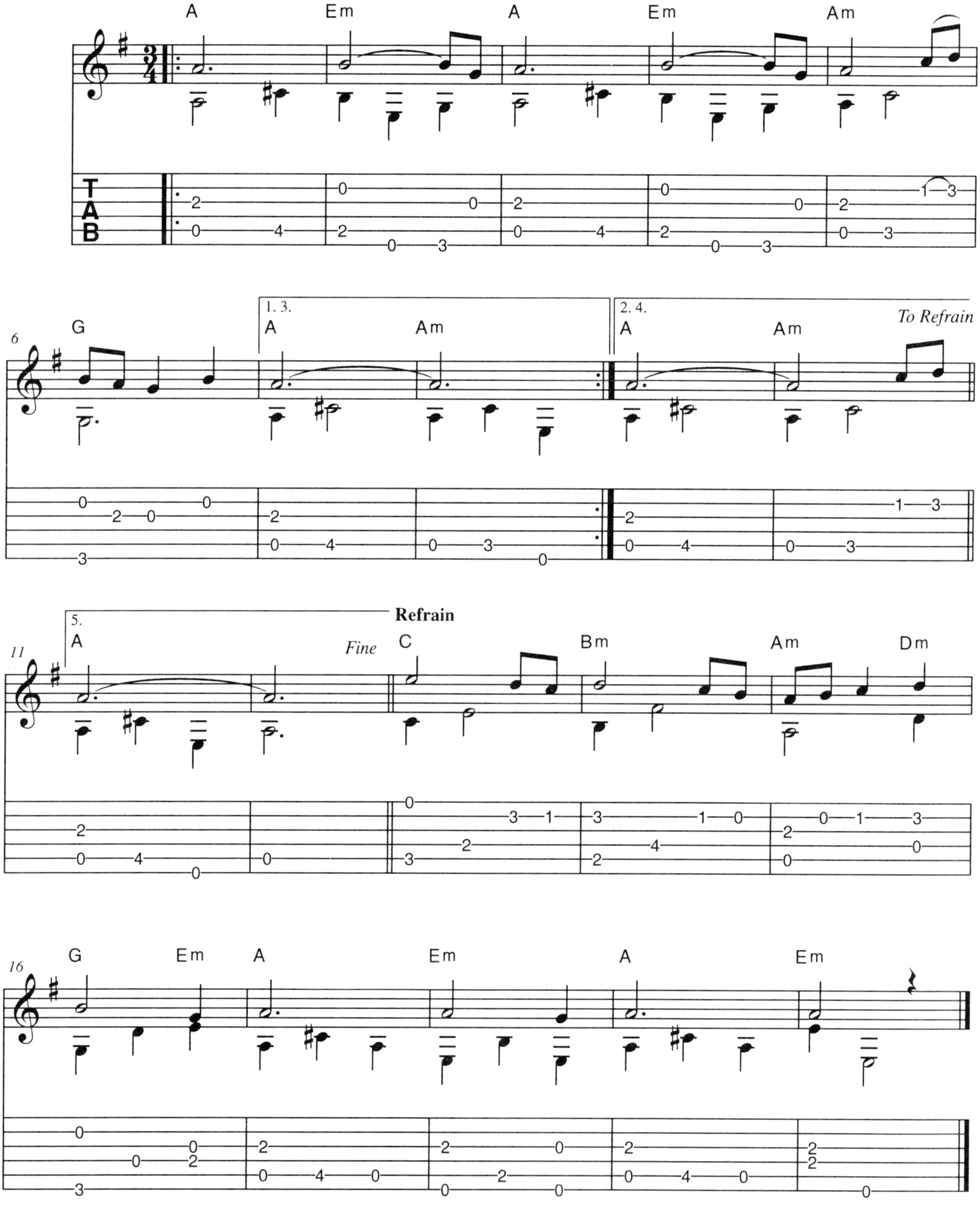

A Em A Em Am

6 G | 1. 3. A Am | 2. 4. A Am *To Refrain*

11 5. A *Fine* | **Refrain** C Bm Am Dm

16 G Em A Em A Em

1. Worthy and holy,
   Let all creation sing Your praise.

2. Beauty in splendor,
   All glory and honor to the Lamb.

CHORUS
For in vast realms of power
You rule the heavens and earth!
Hosanna, Hosanna.

3. Worthy and holy,
   O Lord just to sit and learn of You

4. Beauty in splendor,
   O Lord let us freely worship You.

CHORUS

5. Worthy and holy,
   Let all creation sing Your praise.

Lord, Reign in Me

Tracks #10 & #11 (backup only)

Brenton Brown

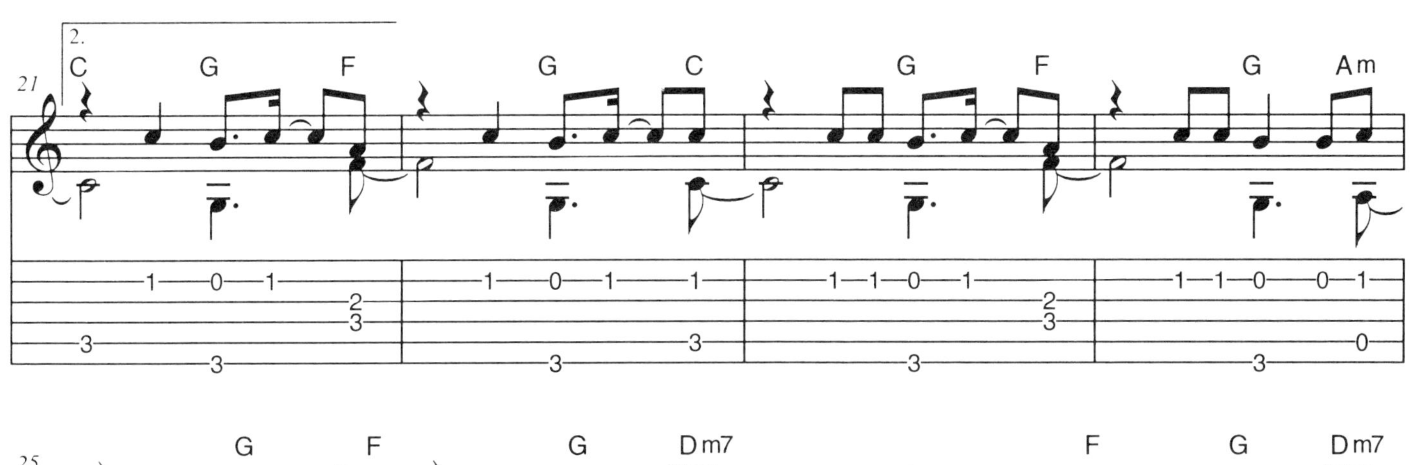

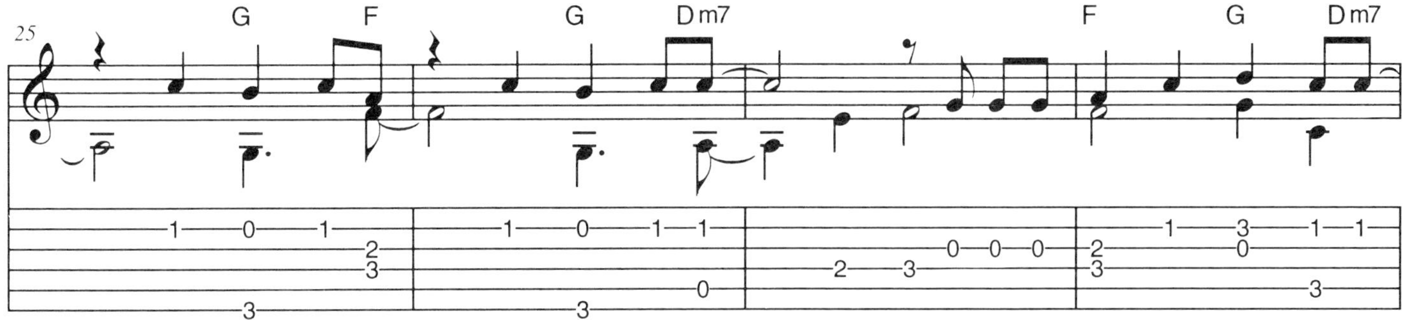

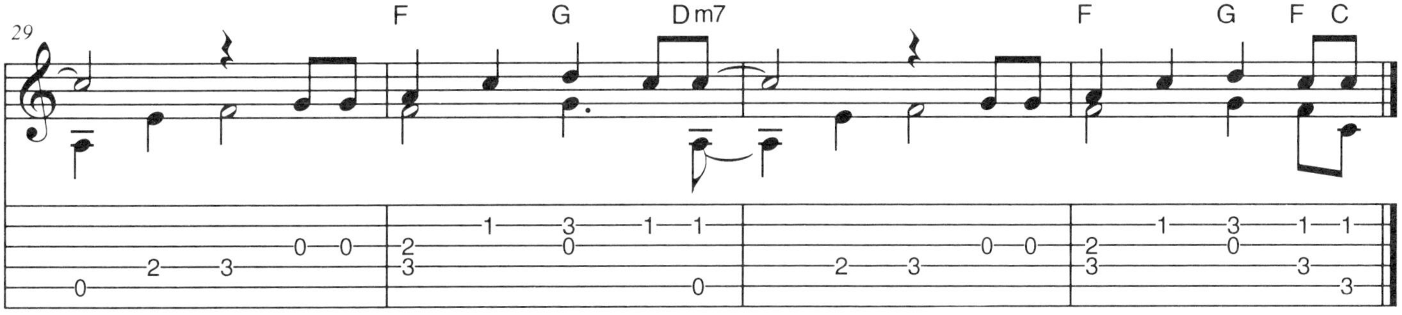

1. Over all the earth,
   You reign on high,
   Every mountain stream,
   Every sunset sky.
   But my one request,
   Lord my only aim
   Is that you reign in me again.

CHORUS

Lord, reign in me,
Reign in your power;
Over all my dreams
In my darkest hour.
You are the lord of all I am,
So won't you reign in me again?

2. Over every thought,
   Over every word,
   May my life reflect
   The beauty of my Lord;
   Because you mean more to me
   Than any earthly thing.
   So won't you reign in me again?

CHORUS

Lord, reign in me,
Reign in your power;
Over all my dreams
In my darkest hour.
You are the lord of all I am,
So won't you reign in me again?
So won't you reign in me again,
So won't you reign in me again?

He Who Comes unto the Lord

Tracks #12 & #13 (backup only)

W. Bay

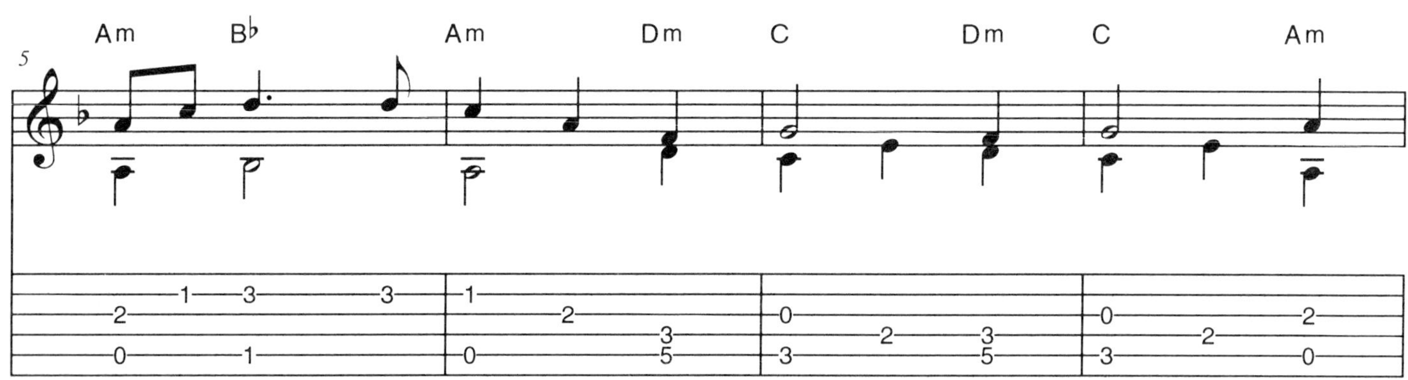

1. He who comes unto the Lord
Never thirsts again,
But from within His soul flows forth
Streams of living water and peace.

2. Those who go forth with the Lord
Dwell in realms of light,
And loving grace flows freely within their lives,
For ever and ever.

3. Those who dwell in fellowship
With the Lord of Lords,
Gain power and strength and to love,
And stand for truth and life.

Come, Now is the Time to Worship

Brian Doerksen

Verses

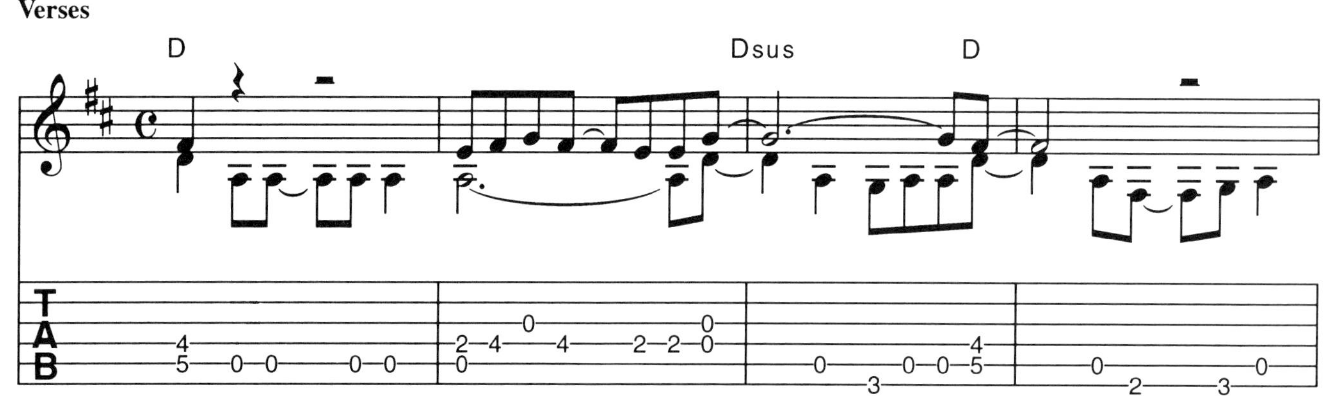

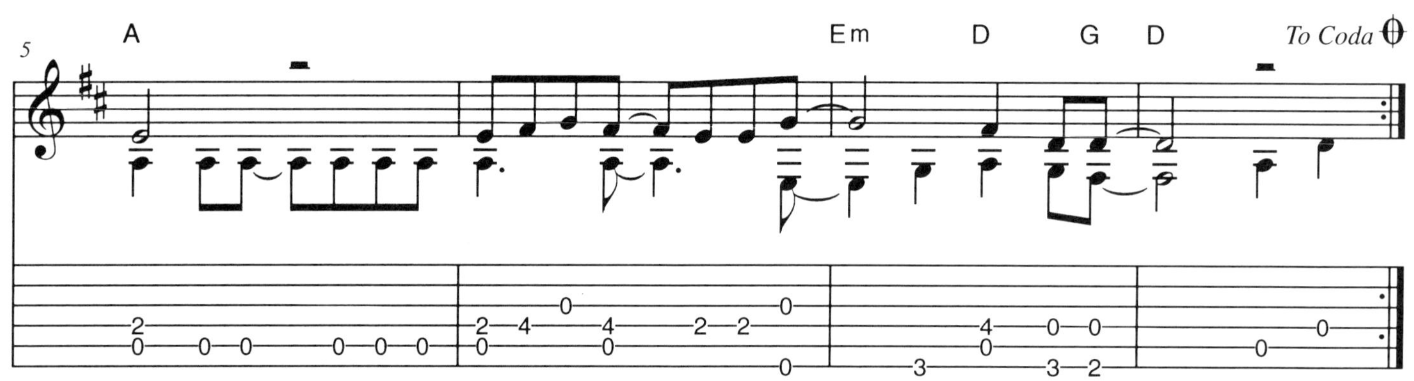

Chorus

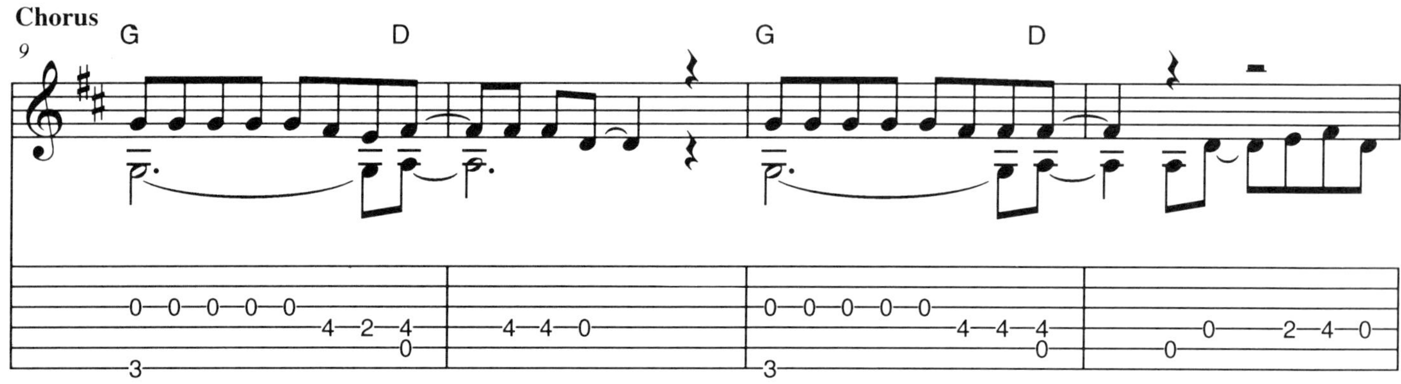

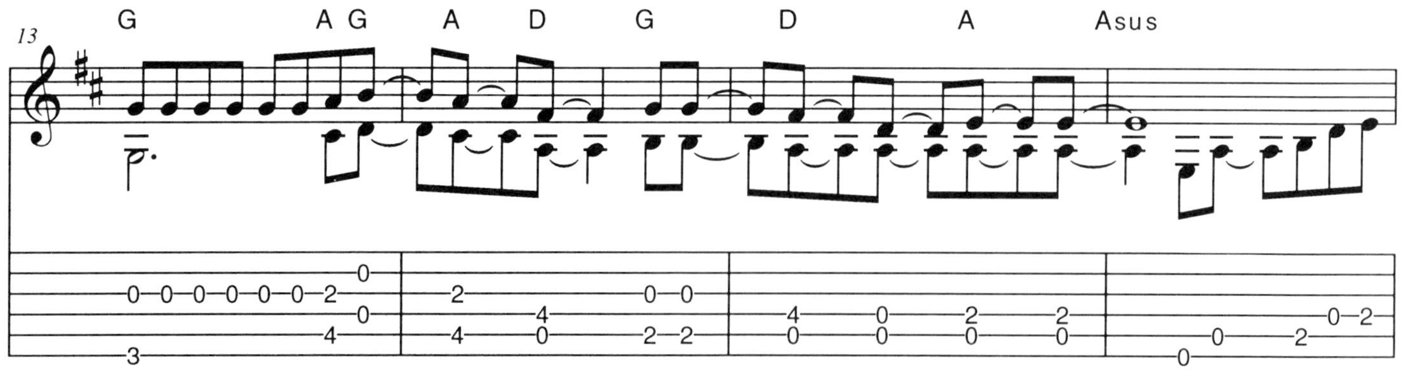

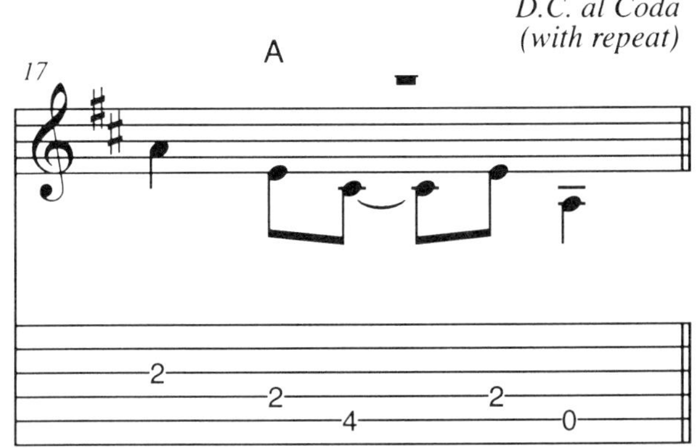

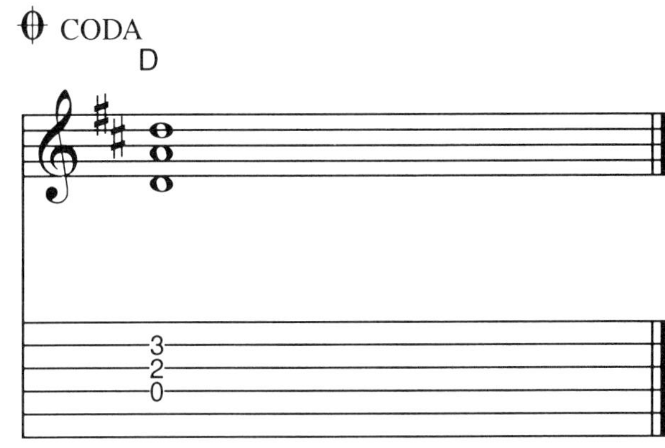

1. Come, now is the time to worship,
   Come, now is the time to give your heart.

2. Come, just as you are to worship,
   Come, just as you are before your God.

CHORUS

One day every tongue will confess You are God.
One day every knee will bow.
Still the greatest treasure remains
For those who gladly choose You now.

1. Come, now is the time to worship,
   Come, now is the time to give your heart

2. Come, just as you are to worship,
   Come, just as you are before God.
   Come.

Draw Me Close

Kelly Carpenter

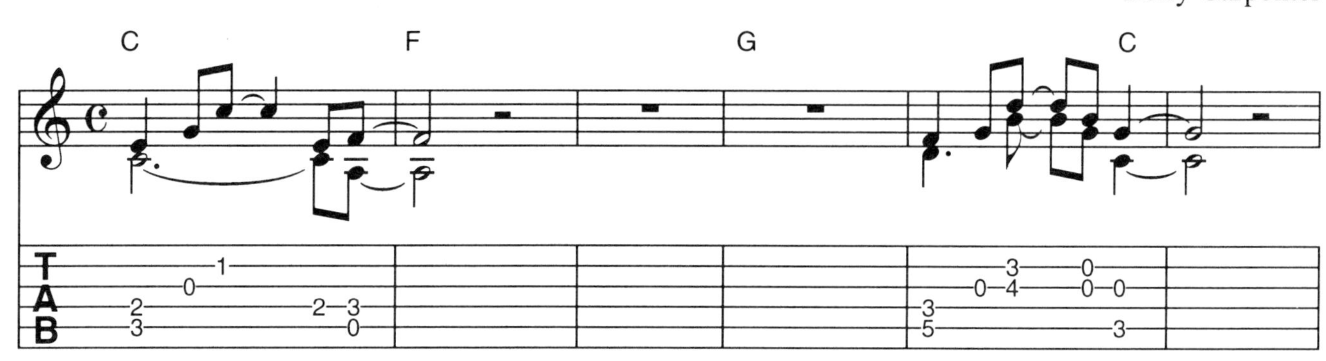

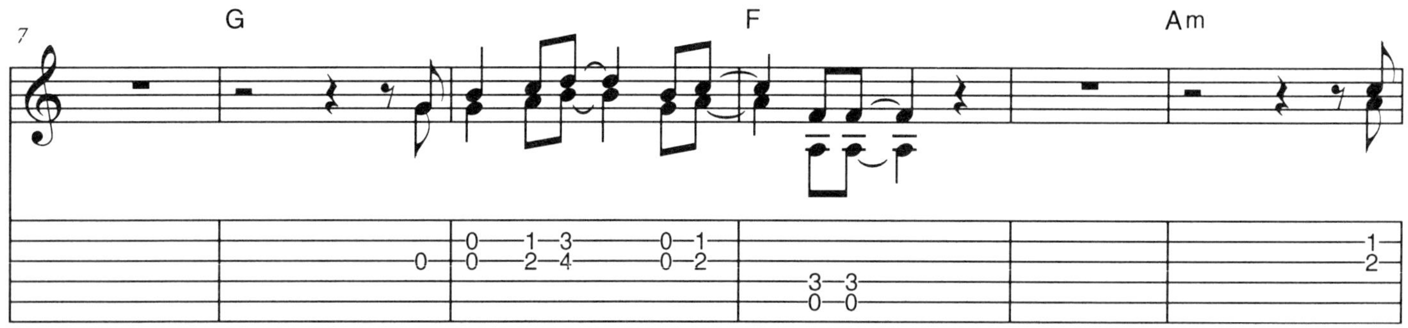

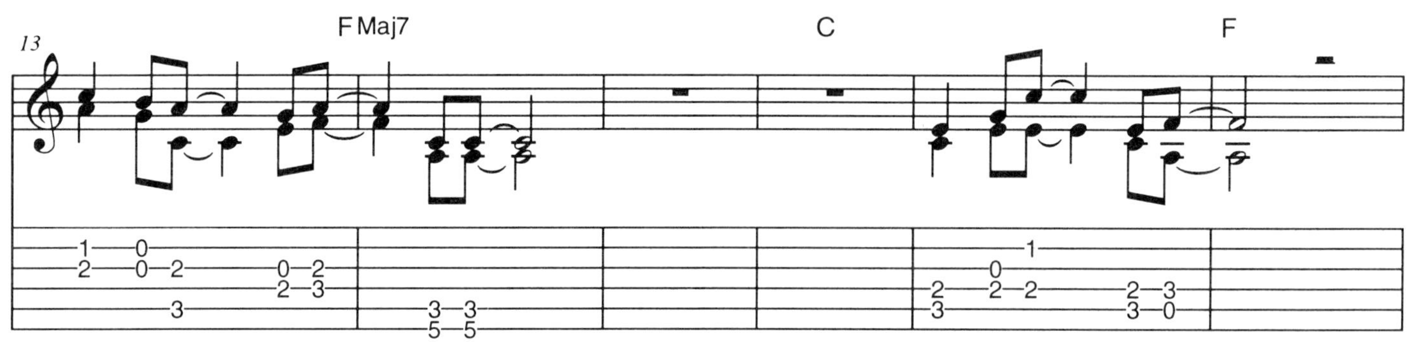

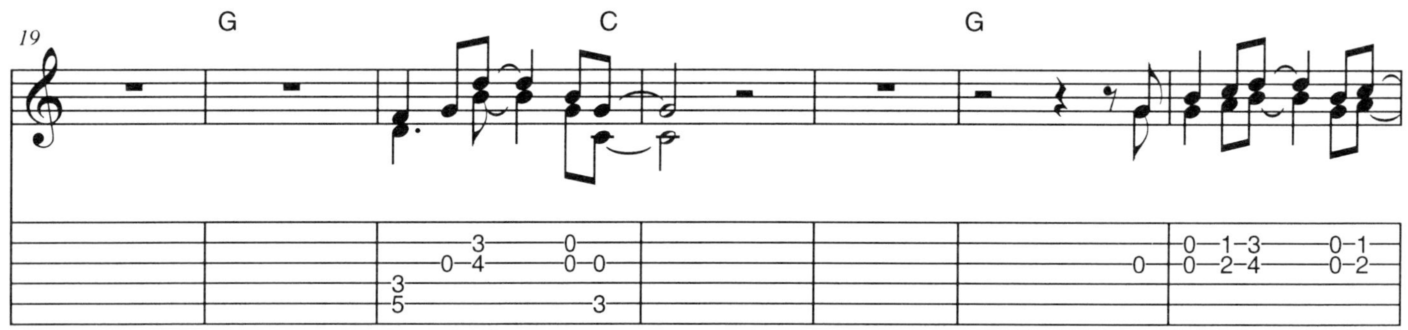

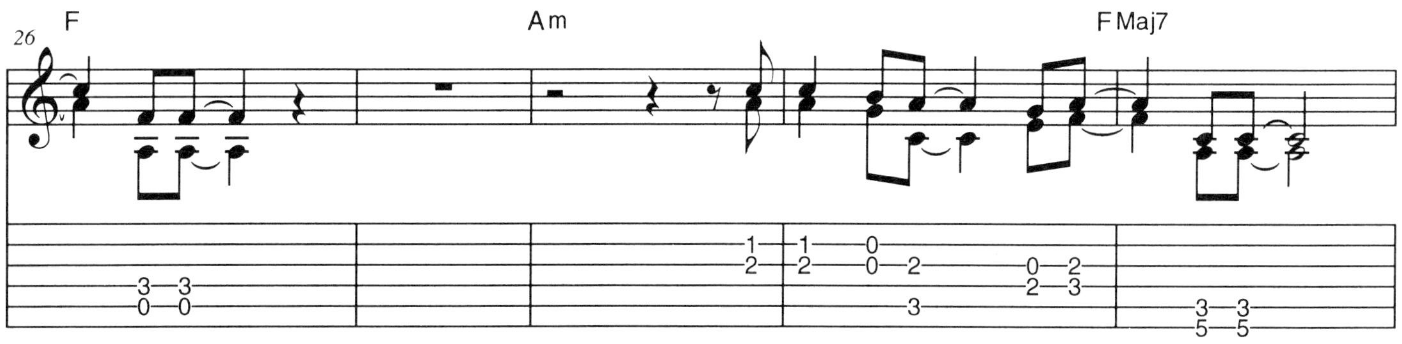

31
C
F
G
C
37
F
G
C
G
F
43
C
G
F
G7sus
G7
48
C
G
F
G7sus
53
G
Am
F
G
C

1. Draw me close to you,
   Never let me go.
   I lay it all down again,
   To hear you say that I'm your friend.

2. You are my desire,
   No one else will do,
   Because nothing else could take your place.

3. To feel the warmth of your embrace,
   Help me find the way,
   Bring me back to you.

4. You're all I want,
   You're all I've ever needed.
   You're all I want,
   Help me know you are near.

We Love Thee, O Lord

W. Bay

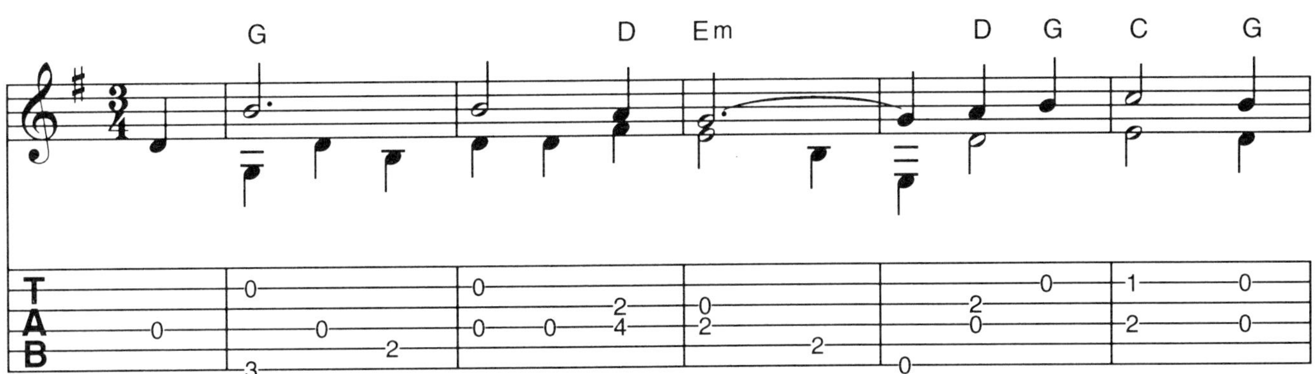

1. We love Thee, O Lord,
   In Your holy habitation,
   And our voice and hearts sing forth
   In praise to Your Holy name.

2. We trust Thee, O Lord,
   In Your word and consultation,
   For to walk with you in steadfast faith
   Is to share Your love.

Holy, Thou Art Holy

Tracks #20 & #21 (backup only)

W. Bay

For accompaniment Chords: Capo 3rd fret and play chords in brackets.

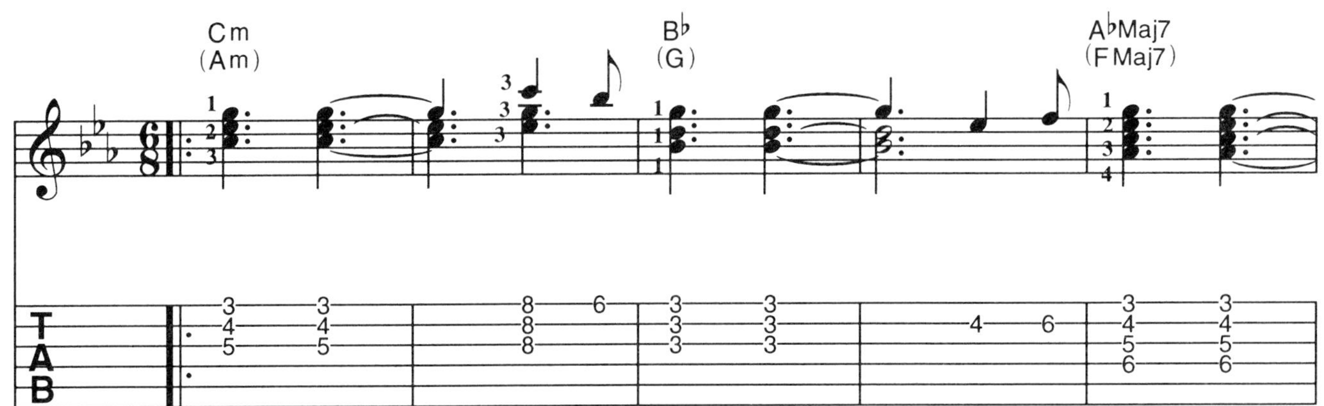

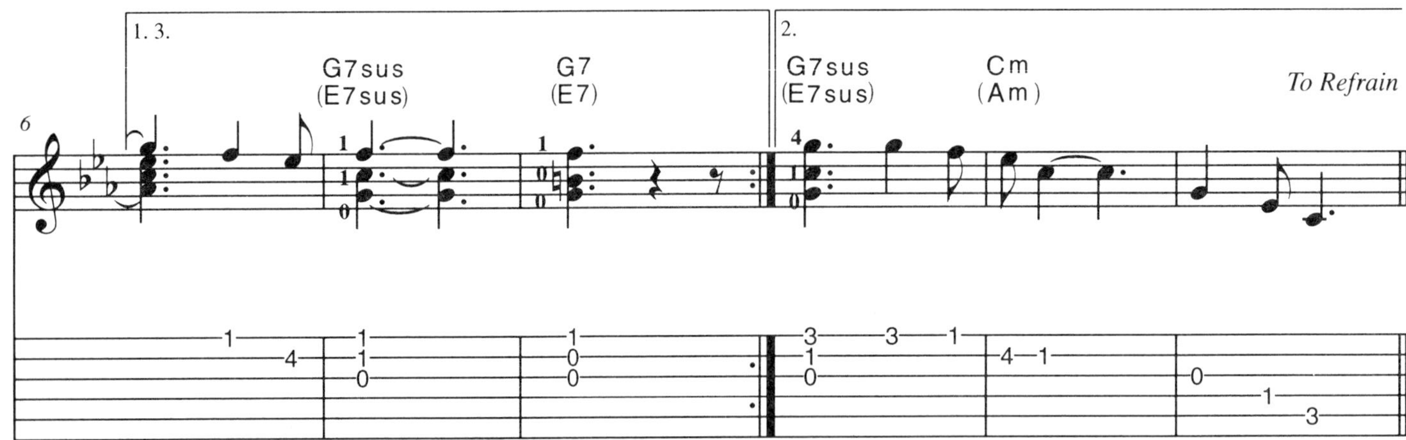

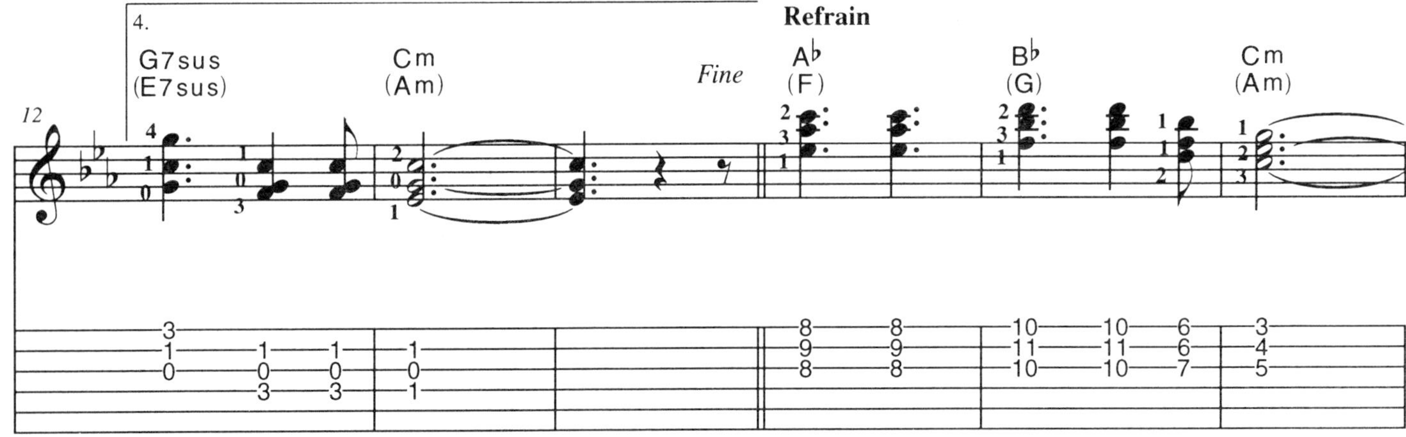

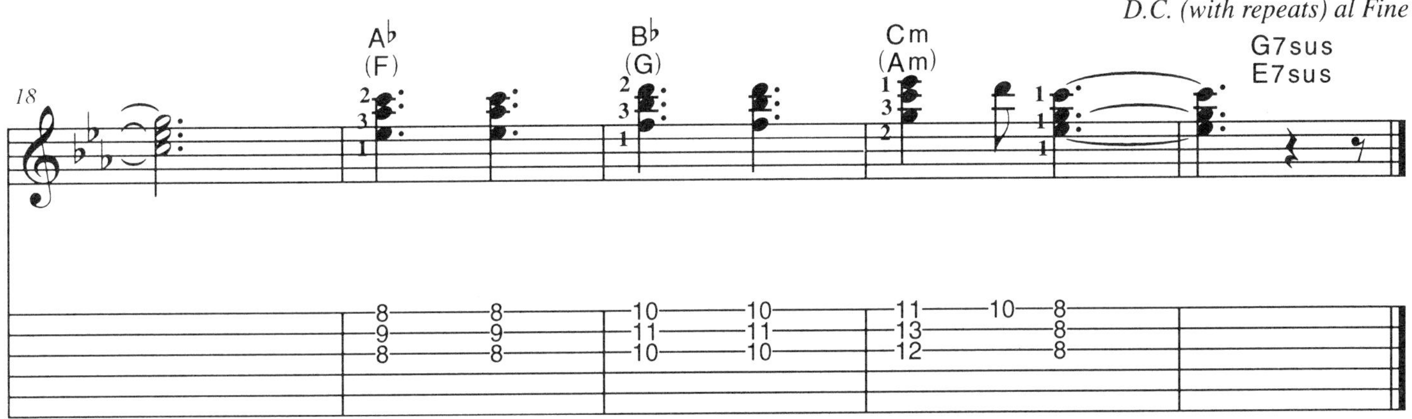

1. Holy, Thou art holy,
   And your splendor fills the skies,

2. Holy, Thou art holy,
   God of power and of might,

Refrain
   Glory, honor, and pow'r!
   All creation worships you!

3. Holy, Thou art holy,
   Let our praises fill the earth,

4. Holy, Thou art holy,
   As we bow before Your throne!

Bless the Lord

W. Bay

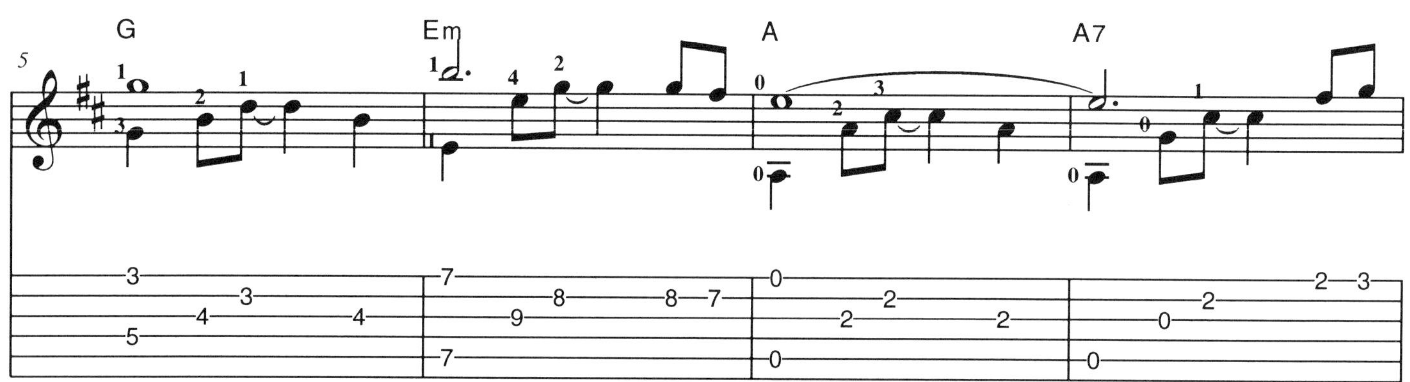

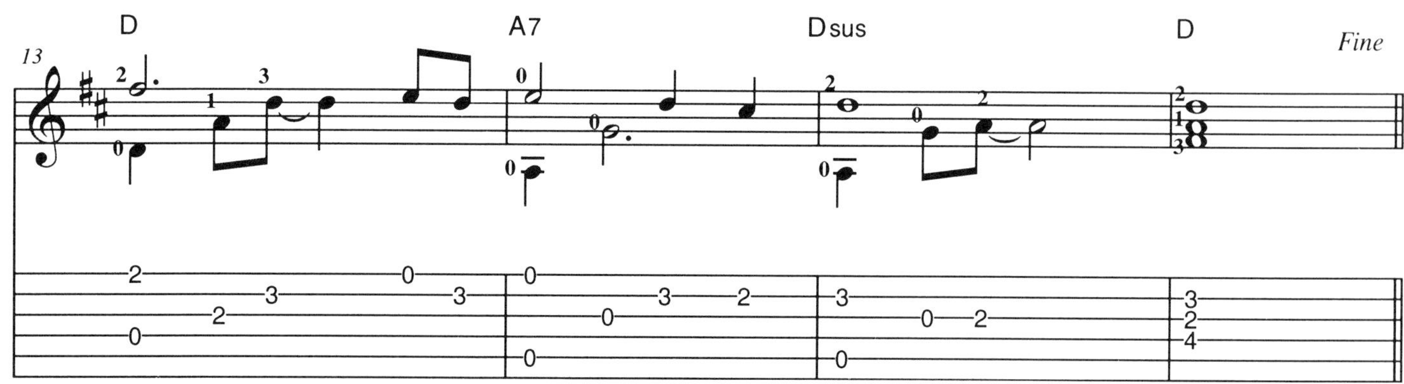

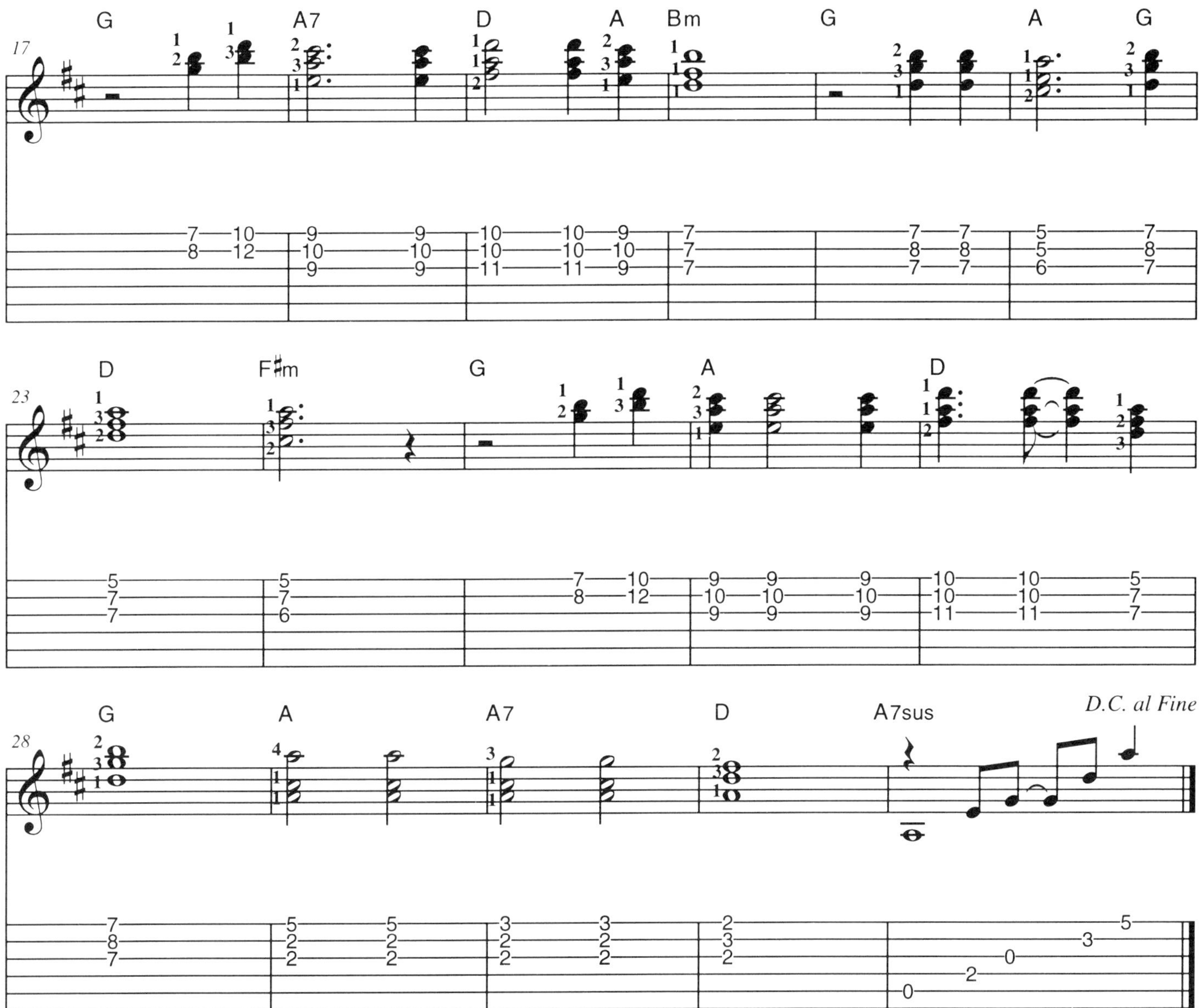

Bless the Lord,
All servants of God,
Lift your hands to the Lord
In His Sanctuary,
Bless the Lord
Who made heaven and earth.
For the Lord has given a new song,
Even praise to God:
Many people shall see it, and fear,
And shall trust in Him.
Bless the Lord,
All servants of God,
Lift your hands to the Lord
In His Sanctuary,
Bless the Lord
Who made heav'n and earth.

Lord, I Lift Your Name on High

Tracks #24 & #25 (backup only)

Rick Founds

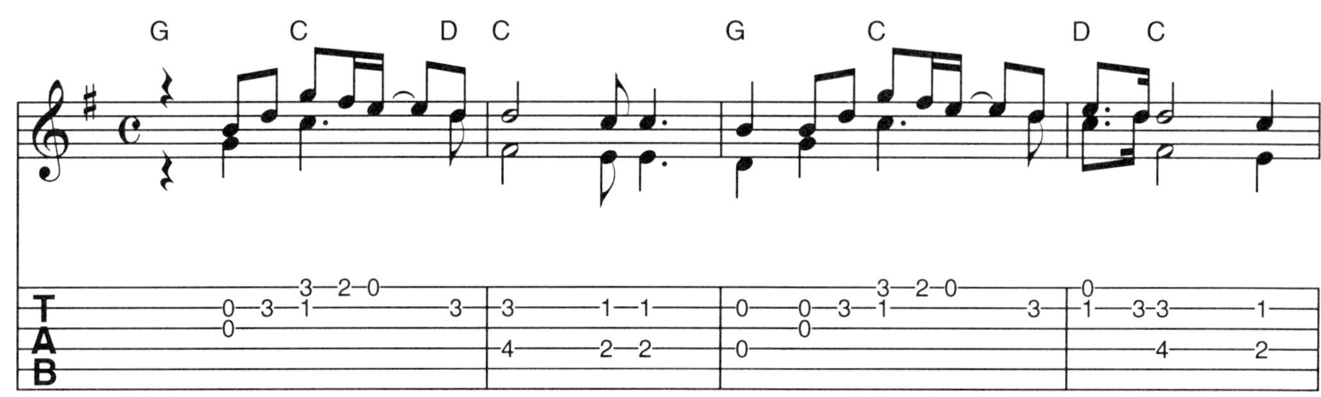

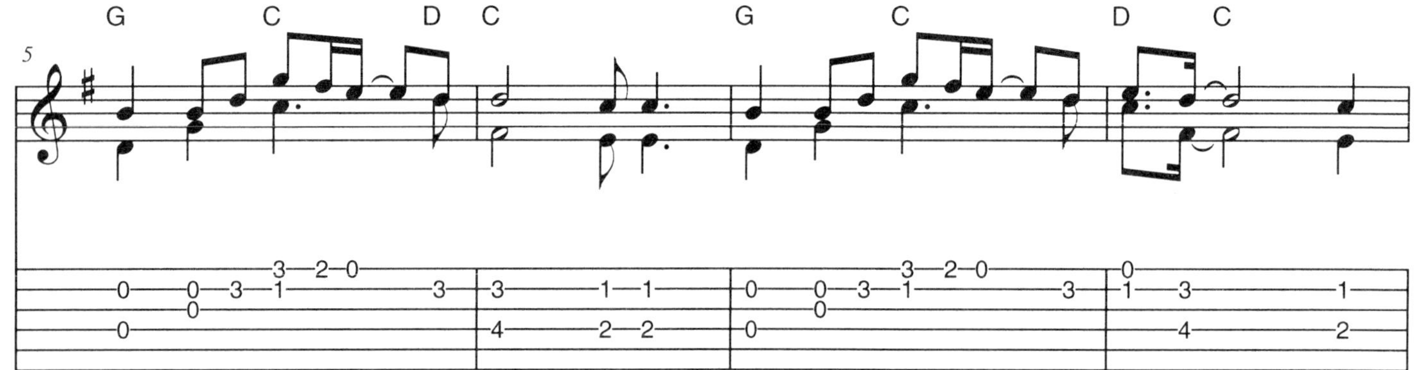

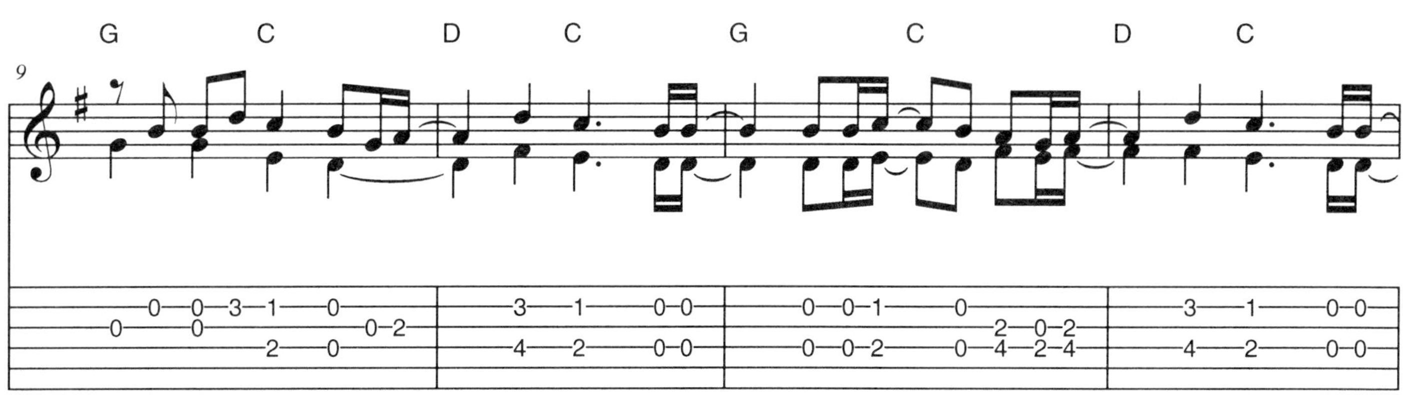

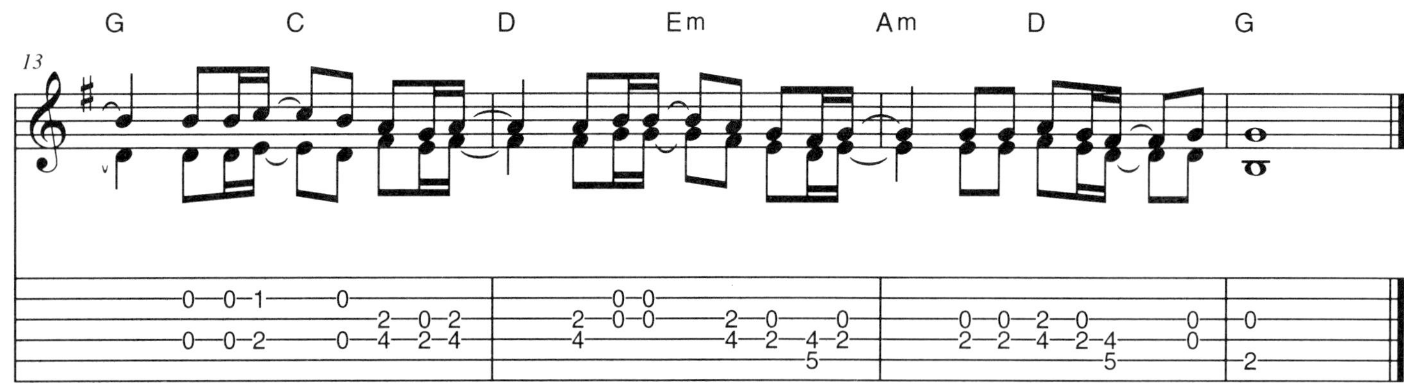

Lord, I lift Your name on high;
Lord, I love to sing Your praises.
I'm so glad You're in my life;
I'm so glad You came to save us.
You came from heaven to earth
To show the way,
From the earth to the cross
My debt to pay;
From the cross to the grave,
From the grave to the sky;
Lord, I lift Your name on high.

As the Deer

Martin Nystrom

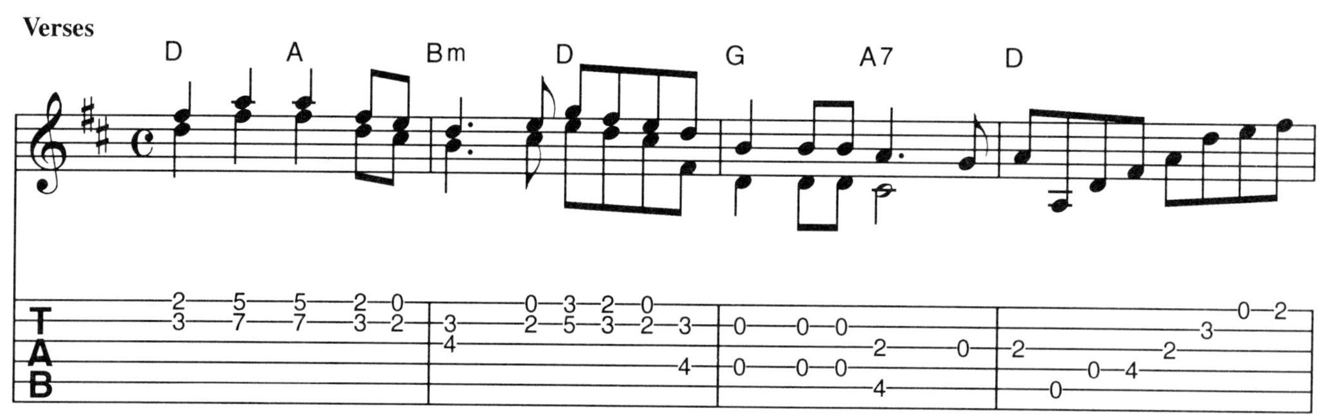

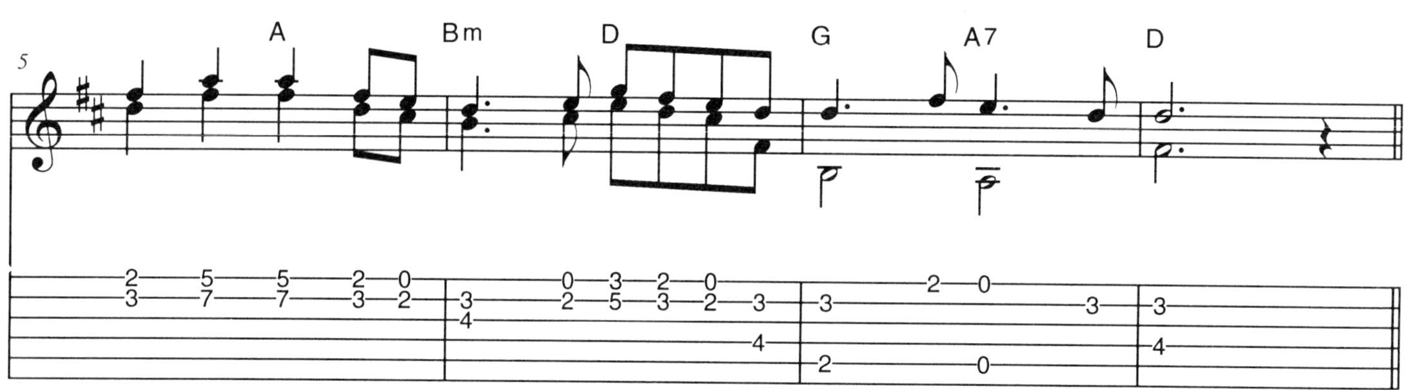

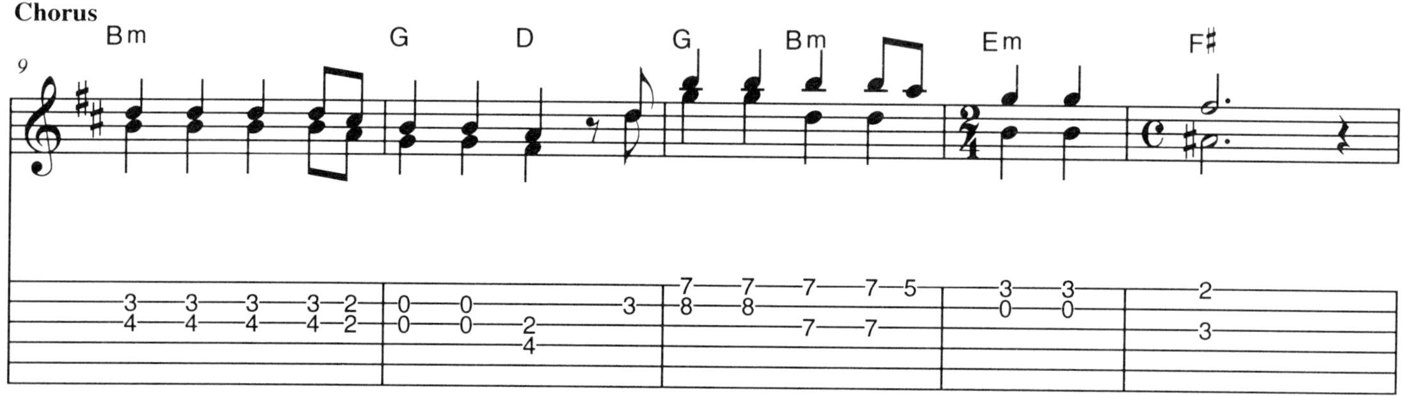

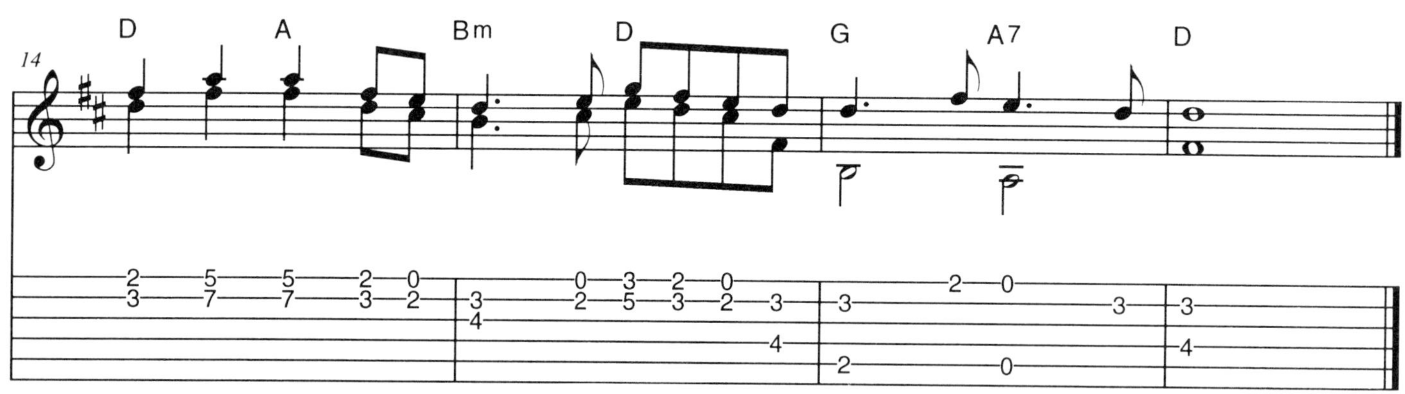

1. As the deer panteth for the water,
   So my soul longeth after Thee.
   You alone are my heart's desire,
   And I long to worship Thee.

CHORUS
   You alone are my strength, my shield;
   To You alone may my spirit yield.
   You alone are my heart's desire,
   And I long to worship Thee.

2. You're my friend and You are my brother
   Even though You are a King.
   I love You more than any other,
   So much more than anything.

CHORUS

3. I want You more than gold or silver,
   Only You can satisfy.
   You alone are the real joygiver
   And the apple of my eye.

CHORUS

Tracks #28 & #29 (backup only)

Give Thanks

Henry Smith

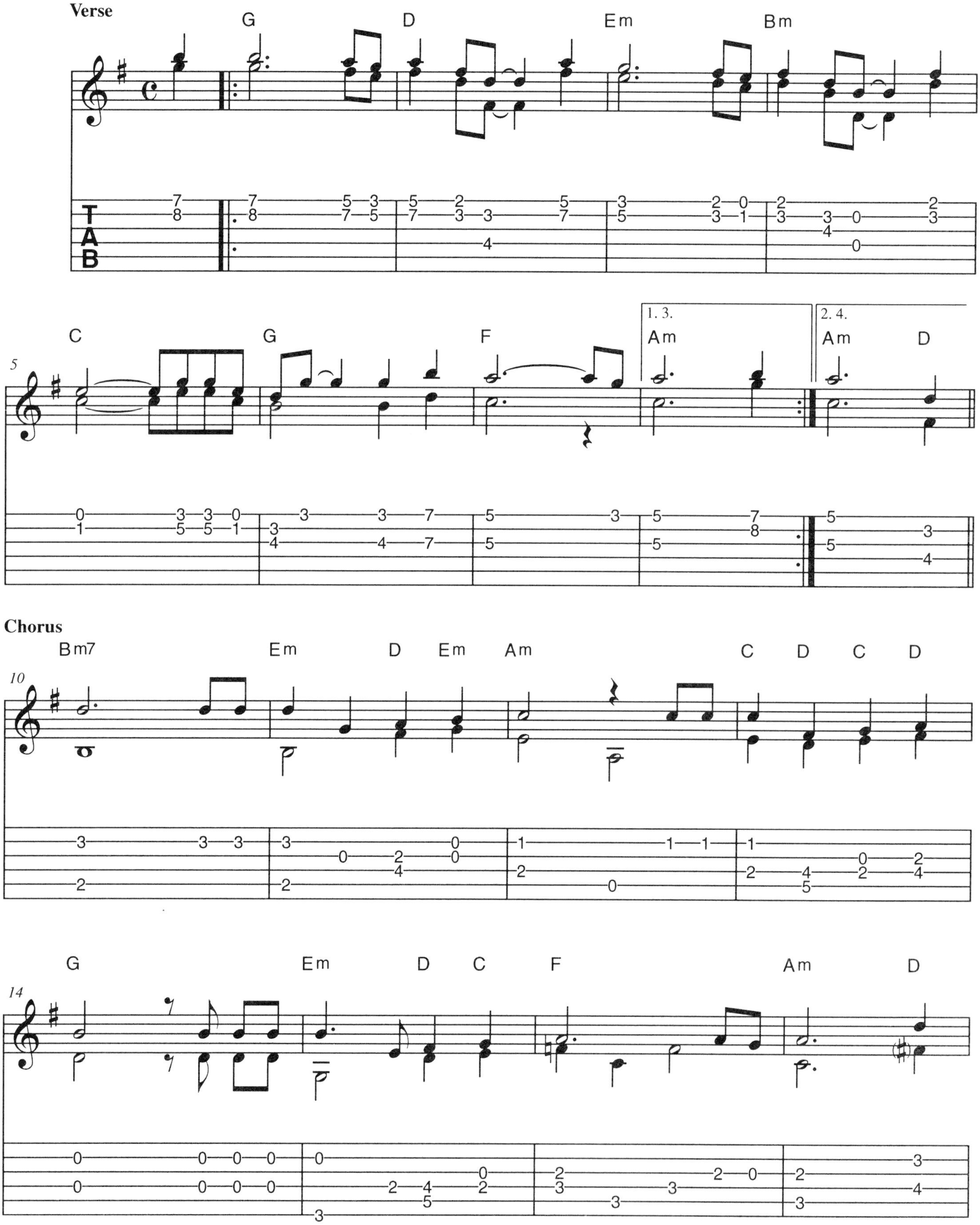

Verse

G D Em Bm

C G F 1. 3. Am 2. 4. Am D

Chorus

Bm7 Em D Em Am C D C D

G Em D C F Am D

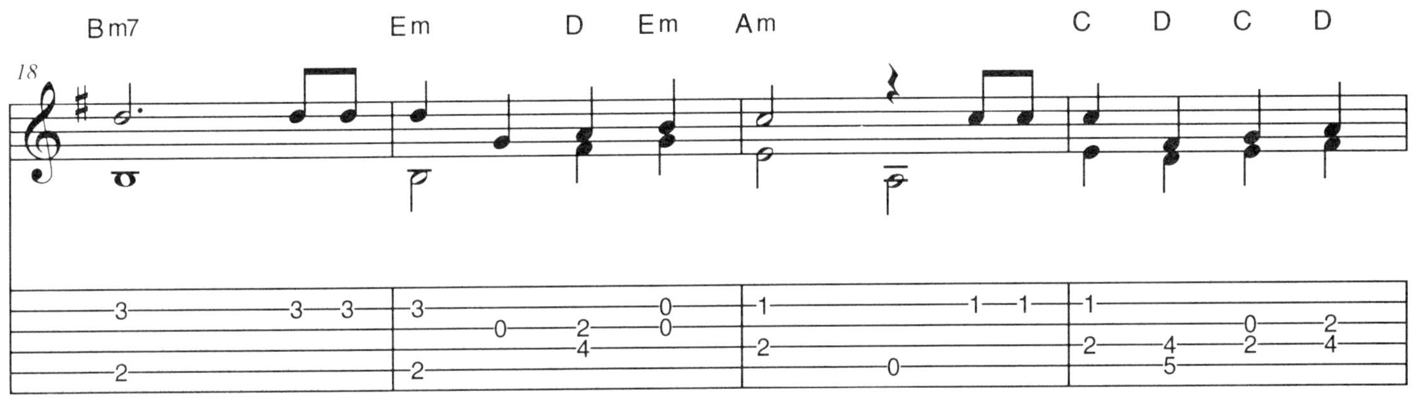

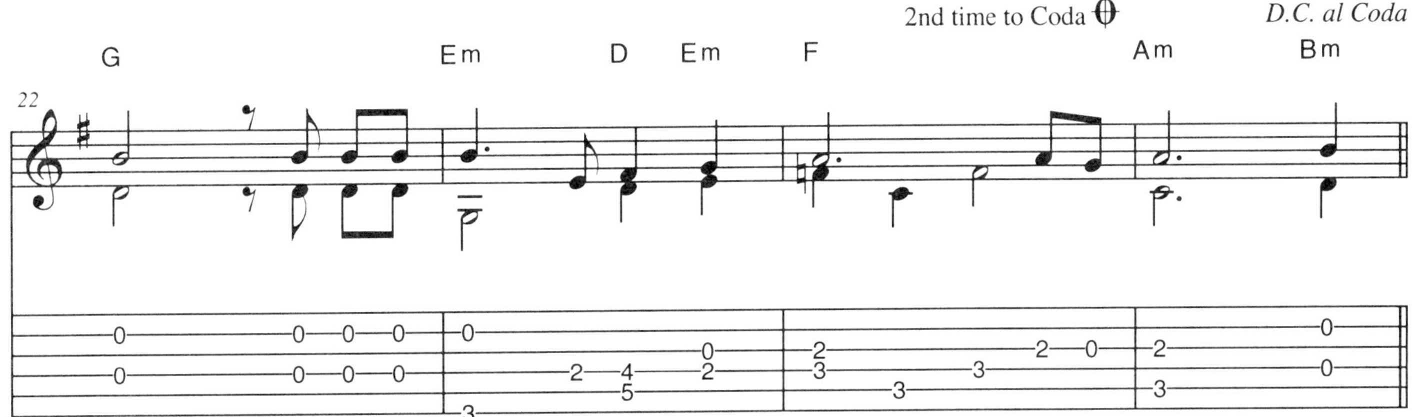

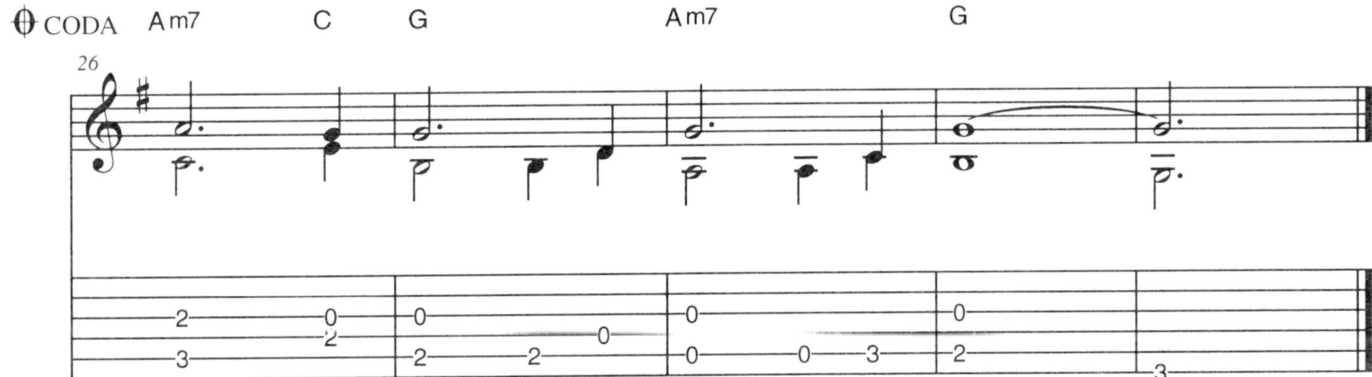

1. Give thanks with a grateful heart,
Give thanks to the Holy One;
Give thanks because He's given
Jesus Christ, His Son.

2. Give thanks with a grateful heart,
Give thanks to the Holy One;
Give thanks because He's given
Jesus Christ, His Son.

Chorus

And now let the weak say, "I am strong,"
Let the poor say, "I am rich"
Because of what the Lord has done for us;
And now let the weak say, I am strong,"
Let the poor say, "I am rich"
Because of what the Lord has done for us.

Final Chorus

And now let the weak say, "I am strong,"
Let the poor say, "I am rich"
Because of what the Lord has done for us;
And now let the weak say, I am strong,"
Let the poor say, "I am rich"
Because of what the Lord has done for us.
Give thanks, give thanks, give thanks.

Jesus, Never Have I Heard a Name

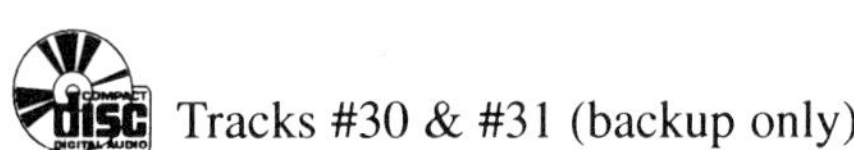

Anonymous

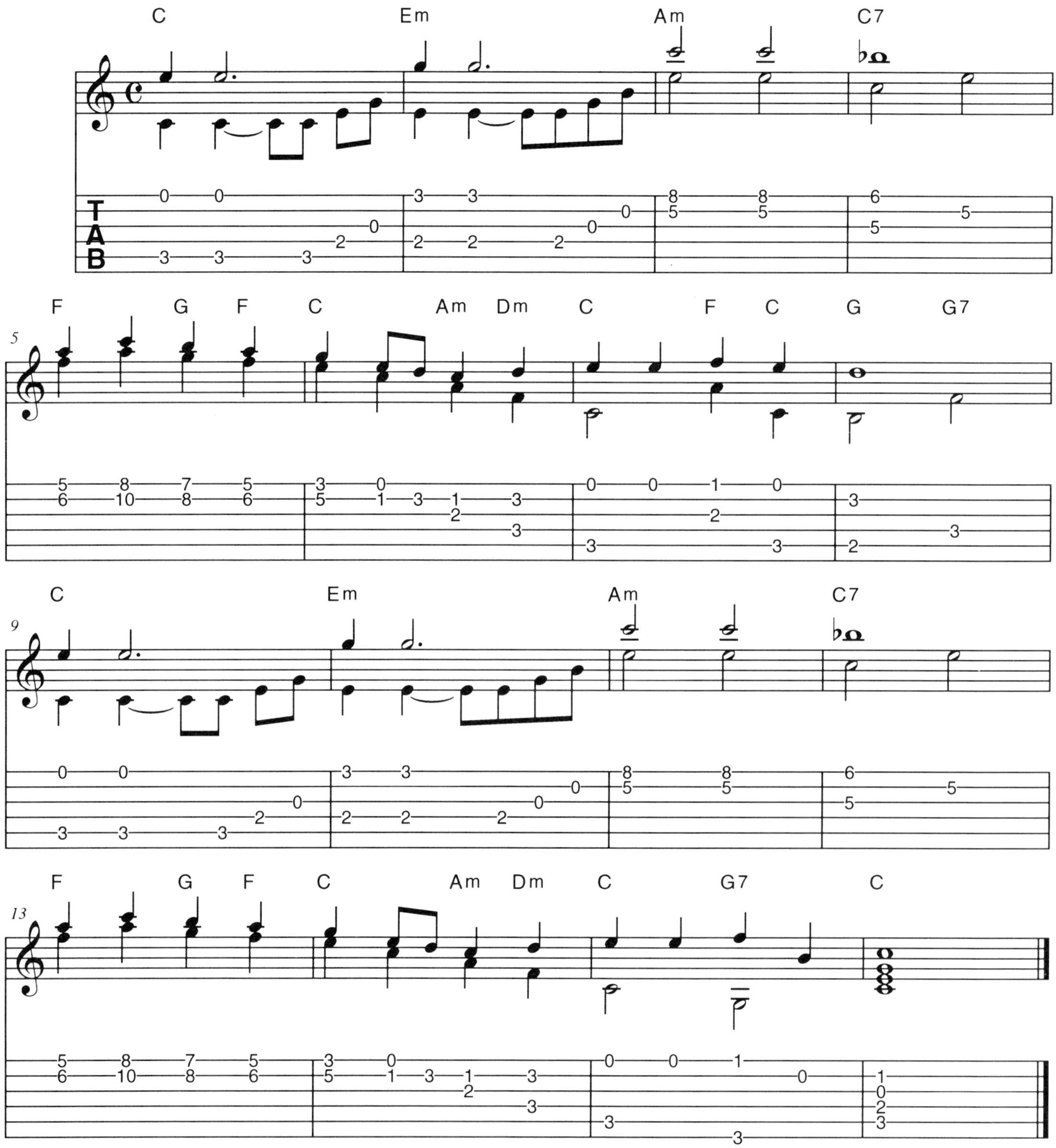

1. Jesus, Jesus, Jesus,
   Never have I heard a name
   That thrills my soul like thine.

2. Jesus, Jesus, Jesus,
   Oh, what matchless grace that links
   That precious Name with mine.